BUY!

MY NEW

BOOK

DOUBLE OR TRIPLE YOUR INCOME AND BUSINESS!

Learn 7 Simple Strategies
All Small Business Owners Should Use
to Reach That Next Level.

JERRY LEVINSON

MY NEW BOOK

Copyright © 2013 by Jerry Levinson

Published by:
Levinson Consulting Group
5Foot6Consulting.com
A Small Family-Owned Business
NO ONE OVER 5'6"

Book design by:
Hollister Design Group
Scottsdale, Arizona

ISBN: 978-0-9899203-0-8

When I was asked who I dedicate this book to, I had to give it some real thought. I love my wife, my kids, and my whole family. I'm grateful for my close friend Jim Mac Millan. Without him I don't know how I would get half the things done that I do. I greatly appreciate Brandi Hollister and the Hollister Design Group for designing my cover and helping me get this book to print.

I have had amazing experiences with my local Master Mind group at Arizona Marketing Association. Chuck Trautman has been one of my greatest mentors in the past two years. Dan Kennedy, Joe Polish, and Chet Holmes have been my favorite gurus to follow and learn from.

The one who I dedicate this book to most is **You!** You're the one making the effort to improve your business and your life. You are the one who will read this book along with others and implement the strategies you learn. You have the wisdom to seek out business coaches, Master Mind groups, and people who can help you on your journey. You are the crazy entrepreneur who is working hard for a better life when the people closest to you are questioning your every move. You plug away and take risks giving other people an opportunity even though you've been advised to "get a safe secure job with benefits."

When you work at building your business and creating wealth, you will also be helping others along the way by giving them opportunities to grow and succeed. I look forward to crossing paths with you on your journey.

To Your Success,
Jerry Levinson

CONTENTS

WARNING!!!

When you read this book I hope you'll be able to distinguish between great advice and smart aleck comments.

See, growing up my mother was Jewish, and my Dad was a Smart Ass. Which makes me a Jewish Smart Ass. For instance, we tell our kids every December, "If you don't behave we'll tell Santa your Jewish."

This also explains the title of **My New Book**. I always thought if I wrote a book I would call it **My New Book**, that way anytime someone went on a talk show or they promoted their book they would say, "Buy My New Book", and they will be talking about my book.

In my window covering business our saying is, "We are a small family-owned business (NO-ONE OVER 5'6")."

I do love using humor and making people laugh, but more important to me is the response we get from our customers. They use us because we are a family-owned business and we are short. People like us, trust us and use us because of a cute saying. We also offer, "Free Snow Shoveling in Phoenix AZ," where the low temperature in the winter is 40 degrees.

A LITTLE ABOUT ME...

I was born in 1969 in Phoenix AZ. My parents had six boys. I think they had so many kids because my dad loves a great deal and the hospital gave him a discount for all the repeat business. My oldest brothers and youngest brothers are twins. I'm an original recipe not to be duplicated or imitated.

My wife and I have four kids. I like to tell my parents that "your six kids don't make our four any easier to raise." We have one son who is currently serving in Afghanistan, and three daughters who we adopted. Our first daughter came from Vietnam. She's just about as beautiful a kid as one could be. My other two daughters we got from Colorado. They are birth sisters. I started my business with my wife but soon after we started having kids we realized that full-time mom was going to be her job. Even though I'm the one who is out every day conducting business and dealing with employees and customers we all know she's the one with the most difficult job.

WHY I WROTE THIS BOOK

In 2008 things were really falling apart. The economy was coming down hard. Businesses were closing left and right. The "Big Anchor" tenants were closing up as well. Our showroom was in a dead center and business was tough. Creditors were cutting credit lines and demanding payments in full. I was half-a-million in debt and couldn't see any way out of it. I tried going thru Take Charge America to help pay off my debts. (If you are in trouble you should try them out. They are a fantastic non-profit company.) It was like swimming upstream. The only way out was to file bankruptcy.

I'm grateful we have that mechanism to start over. I'm not proud of having to file but it was a ginormous relief and an opportunity to start over.

I'm not a big fan of bad moods, especially my own. I had to get out of the funk I was in. My wife had some CDs from a Tony Robbins seminar. Wow did that change my world. The positive attitude changed my mindset and I went to his website for more. That's where I found Chet Holmes, a business guru who wrote, *The Ultimate Sales Machine*. This is a great book that I recommend to all entrepreneurs. I've captured a lot of Holmes's advice in *My New Book*.

Once you enter this world where you are seeking professional advice it's like a drug that you can't get enough of. Some friends told me about this marketing guy who helps mostly carpet cleaners, Joe Polish. Well it turns out that Joe helps more than carpet cleaners and the best part is he's right in my backyard in Tempe, AZ. Joe's done so well teaching entrepreneurs how to do excellent marketing that he now runs a very high-level Master Mind group called 25K Group. It's named that because it cost $25,000 a year to belong. You must do One Million a year to be a member. You can check out his free podcasts at www.Ilovemarketing.com.

At an I Love Marketing event Joe introduced Dan Kennedy. Dan was Joe's mentor. Now I'm in planet Dan, GKIC Marketing, and I belong to an Executive Master Mind group in Arizona held by Chuck Trautman.

If you are in the Phoenix area I would encourage you to check out Chuck Trautman's monthly Master Mind meetings at ArizonaMarketingAssociation.org. I would love to see you there and talk about your business and your marketing strategies. Chuck has been a great mentor and friend. The best thing about all these gurus is not that they dispense with the best advice, it's that they bring the best most interesting, brilliant marketers to the table to help.

Entrepreneurs: We are in an exclusive club of men and women who work hard at finding out the best marketing solutions to growing and succeeding in our business. Problems and challenges are opportunities to make things better. Our family and friends often times don't understand the seemingly stupid things we try. But we are the risk takers. We are the ones who are going to try, and we are the ones who will fail, learn, and move on. Failure is a part of life and business and it won't detour us from trying even harder. We ignore the voices of the masses in order to improve life for our families, friends, and our communities. We have a passion and a love for life and we are determined to constantly learn and grow to make our lives the best it can be. I hope you are a crazy, misunderstood and relentless entrepreneur as well. We need more of you out there and I look forward to meeting every one of you.

When I took the time to learn about marketing, sales, and business operations that's when everything started to change. My business started increasing, and more importantly my profits were going up. I was able to hire sales people, office staff, and I was able to increase my prices. I was "working on my business" instead of "working in it."

There are a lot of experts out there. You should find the one who speaks best to you and your needs. The saying is, "When the student is ready the teacher will appear." That is a true saying, and when you are ready to go to the next level your mentor will be there for you.

Big Lesson: Even though everyone was going thru the same thing I was—bankruptcy, laying off employees, closing their doors—I knew my failure was my fault. I owned it. Two things I realized: 1. If you blame an outside force for your failures than you have to rely on an outside force to change your situation, and, 2. I wasn't willing to give up that much control over my life to something I couldn't control, such as the economy or elections. I also knew if I understood how to run a business better I could have avoided the debt and bankruptcy. If you are an excellent technician, that's great, but it's not enough to own and run a successful business. My chiropractor friend was telling me of Charlie, a guy who runs a much more successful practice than he does because he understands marketing, sales, business operations, how to fill each position with the best employees, how to give those employees the tools they need to be successful; and he will do what it takes to grow his practice and be successful. Meanwhile he's fat and out-of-shape and he wasn't top of his class, quite frankly he's not even a good chiropractor. My friend is an excellent chiropractor. He runs a good business but not nearly as good as Charlie. Charlie built his business for success. He has great profits and he employs more than 10 people, giving them good employment and benefits. Charlie has also built a business using systems that can be duplicated. He can open up other offices, which is his plan, and he can sell his business someday for a great amount of money.

WHY DID YOU GET INTO BUSINESS IN THE FIRST PLACE?

Most of us got into business because we have skills in a certain area. If you are a plumber or an electrician it's probably easy and fun for you because it comes naturally.

People take a lot of pride in being a smart, reliable, professional technician. It's a great feeling to know that you can do a job better than anyone and that so many people appreciate your knowledge and hard work. I love coming up with solutions for my customers for their window covering needs. I really love it when they have a problem that no one can figure out but me. My customers have a lot of respect and appreciation for me and what I do.

This is the reason you got into business in the first place. You are so good at what you do and you have a desire to take better care of your customers than your employer did. You also thought, *"Huh, why am I working so hard to make someone else money? I can open up my own place and keep all the profits for myself."*

THE REAL PROBLEM

The real problem is that there are only so many hours in a day. You can only take care of so many customers and handle so many problems all by yourself. You are limited by the clock.

There is a BIG DIFFERENCE between being a great technician and a great business person.

When I started to let go of the things that I knew I could do really well—such as installing blinds or selling products—I slowly began to trust others to do a great job. I quickly began to realize how great it was to make money even though I never met the customers. You'll experience the same euphoria I did when you leave on vacation for a week and your employees are still making you money.

You are going to love being able to provide excellent service to your customers even though you are hanging out with your kids on a Saturday afternoon.

BEST DAY EVER

I was in Vegas one summer on a vendor provided vacation. I got a call from the office to let me know we closed three jobs that day that totaled $65,000 dollars. Now, in my business $65,000 is a pretty good month. We did that in a day; and the best part, I was in Vegas at the time.

HERE'S WHAT YOU SHOULD LEARN WHEN YOU READ
MY NEW BOOK

I'm going to show you *How To Make The Buying Process Easy* for your customers. That's right, we want to talk about ways that you can simplify what you do so you can make the buying decision easy for your customers. Many business people don't realize how tough they make it on their customers to make a decision.

I want to show you *How to Get the Most Money for Your Products and Services*, and get more customers while raising your prices. If you value your skills, time, knowledge, and efforts, you should be able to command more money for what you do.

You are going to learn *How to Close More Sales* with strategies that any sales person will be comfortable using. Chet

Holmes teaches, "If you believe you have the right product and service for your customers, then you have an obligation to close as hard as you can!"

You are going to learn some *Killer Marketing Strategies* and *How to Find Your Best Customer*. Who are your best customers? These are the clients who will pay you the most for your services and who will be raving fans. You want customers who will share what you do with all of their friends.

I'm going to show you *The Best Way to Grow Your Business* by hiring good people, and how to lay down the proper systems and expectations to get the best results from your employees.

You'll also learn *How to Get the Most Out of Your Employees and Yourself* by holding weekly meetings. This is one thing small business people are most reluctant to do, but if you take the time and effort to have weekly meetings, they will make the largest impact on the success of your business.

Now let's *Put It All Together* and discuss how important it is to have the right attitude. You can't have real success without the right mindset. How do you truly reach success?

MAKE THE BUYING PROCESS EASY

Product Strategies

Okay... let's dive right in here with one of my favorite topics. It's probably one of the easiest things to do and it's something that most business owners struggle with.

NARROW YOUR CUSTOMER'S CHOICES

I've become a big fan of a lot of these new business TV shows like *Undercover Boss, Bar Rescue, Restaurant Impossible* and *Car Lot Rescue*. If you haven't watched these shows I would recommend them to you as a business person.

In one episode of *Undercover Boss*, someone in my industry, window coverings, was the Boss. He was tagging along with a Franchisee/salesman to a customer's home. When the sales-person met with the couple he gave them a whole book showing them all their choices for window coverings. He asked their opinion of which designs and styles they liked best and to eliminate the ones they didn't like. He showed them ALL the window coverings they would have to choose from therefore making the buying decision very difficult for the customer.

What he should have done was interview the customer. How

important is privacy to you? Do you need a window covering that insulates very well? What did you have before? Did you like it? How long do you plan to stay in this home? Will you be painting your house or do you prefer to keep the colors you currently have? Why do you want to cover your windows?

Let's find out what our customers wants, needs, and desires are. Then let's be the professional and recommend the treatment that will suit their needs the best. Maybe you give them two choices and you explain why you would recommend each treatment.

In the window covering industry there are a lot of options as to the controls the blinds will have. For instance we have a product called a Duette. That shade comes in semi-opaque or a black-out. There are a ton of colors and fabrics to choose from such as a ¾" or a 1 ¼" pleated shade. There are Ultra-Glide controls, LiteRise, EasyRise, or Standard. Now if you give your customer all these choices, chances are the customer will get confused or frustrated and may decide not to buy.

Before the customer had all of these choices it was much easier for you to sell, and for that customer to make the decision to buy. To best serve your customer you should present the options that will work best. If you did your job right in finding out what the customer's wants and needs were, you will be able to **make it easier for your customer to buy!**

When we became a Hunter Douglas Gallery showroom we were given all these great new products to sell that our competition didn't have. It was exciting to have so many great options for our customers. But we quickly realized that we were selling better before we had all those new options. We were making it difficult for our customers to decide by giving them too many choices. We were also making it very difficult for us to sell because for every product you would have to look at all the variables, such as minimum or maximum width and height. Then if a customer was interested, you were stuck pricing out multiple options. Our closing rates were going down because we made it tough for our customer to buy.

"A CONFUSED MIND TAKES NO ACTION"

If you give people too many choices, often times they make the decision *not to decide* and you are left without a sale. If you've ever been in a Costco you will notice that they only give their customers two choices, and sometimes only one.

It's funny as adults we don't like making decisions. You may ask your spouse, "Where do you want to go to dinner?" not because you are being nice and letting her decide, but because you don't want to have to decide. How many times do we, as parents, ask our kids where they want to go eat? I'm guilty of this myself. You have a 10 year-old kid in the back of your mini-van playing with her Barbie Doll and you are asking her where the family should go to eat. I don't know why but it's human nature, we just don't like making decisions.

On the Food Network shows, *Bar Rescue* and *Restaurant Impossible,* one of the things they do is shorten the menu. *Instead of giving the customer so many different choices and so many different price points, let's just Kick Ass at making four dishes. We will be famous for our Fried Chicken. Or we will be known as the best Margarita bar on the strip.*

There's this Philly cheese steak restaurant in Tempe called Fore Fathers. All they do is make Philly Cheese Steaks. These guys opened up their doors a few years ago and immediately they were packed every day at lunch. *How is that?* How can you only serve one type of food and beat Denny's or I-Hop or a big chain that has all the marketing and big menus where you can have anything you want? I know you've gone into these restaurants before and everything on the menu looks good, and what happens? You can't decide what you want, and when you do decide the food is usually not as good as how it looks on the menu. *Why is that?* It's because they are trying to do too many things to try and please too many people.

Look at the franchises who are doing well right now: Chick-Fil-A, In & Out Burger, FatBurger – just to name a few. What do all these places have in common? They have a small menu. If you go into any of these restaurants you can make up your mind pretty quick, you are less stressed, and they can focus on doing a great job because it's a very simple system.

I purchased a commercial on cable TV and they broke down the cost of the commercial:

Writing the script	**$150**
Editing	**$75**
Filming	**$97**
Running the ad	**$70 / 30-second spot**

They had about seven more charges on their invoice. Immediately I started arguing with their charges. I wrote the script – I did the editing, etc, etc.

If they had come to me and said, "We will run 25 commercials for you for just $2500, and that will include writing the script, editing, filming, and all production costs," I would have probably said, "Let's go for it." Instead they gave me a menu of costs which made it seem as if they were nickel-and-diming me.

When we give an estimate to a customer often times they will ask you to break down the price window-by-window. I teach my sales people to ignore this request the first time and give a customer one price for the entire project. Often times they will go for it because they want their whole project done. If they want it broken down, they will ask again and you can do it for them, but initially give that customer one price for everything they want.

Chances are your industry has constant changes. They will introduce new products, they will raise prices, and they will manufacturer products differently—sometimes better and sometimes worse. You have to constantly learn and keep up with all the industry changes by taking classes or attending webinars or having a meeting with the manufacturer's sales representative.

YOUR CUSTOMER DOES NOT KNOW WHAT YOU KNOW!

Your job is to educate your customers as to what is in their best interests based on your experience and knowledge. Sales people often get nervous when selling to customers. They want them to believe they are honest so they'll explain too much about their widget.

One of my biggest pet peeves is the Internet optimization industry. These guys are usually the worst sellers and the worst business people in an industry. How many times have you talked to somebody who can build you a web site and optimize it for you, but you walked away asking, "What did he just say?" Internet gurus have a desire to explain everything to you. *Why is that?* The Internet is one of the best marketing tools out there but I don't care how it works. It's not about bounce rates, and cookies, and spam — **I WANT CUSTOMERS!**

And I don't care if you plan on throwing monkeys out of an airplane with a parachute with my name and logo on it. Don't tell me how it works, just get me results, get me buying customers. Please do not explain every little detail about what you are going to do for me, because you are going to lose me as a customer.

I just bought a new Toyota Tundra truck. It will tow a boat and I can use it at work. It's comfortable and reliable. I can drive from California to Maine and back without it breaking down. *Do you know why?* Me neither, and I don't care! I want to get

5

in that truck and, when I turn the key, it goes *vroom-vroom* and off I go.

I'd like to know whose bright idea it was to put 350 different paint colors on a sample deck? Can you imagine what would happen if we only had 35 colors to choose from? We would all get our homes painted. I wonder how many couples have walked out of a paint store because they couldn't decide which shade of green would go best with their furniture.

YOUR TURN

If you sell flooring, can you package the pad and installation with the purchase of the carpet? If you are a dentist, wouldn't it be better to sell someone your "Clean For Life" package that has them coming back every six months for cleaning? If you are a pool builder, can you give your customer a remodeling package that includes the patio and overhang and backyard landscape? Can you give them one price and give them every-thing they want rather than breaking down the cost of tear out, building the foundation, inserting the tile, etc.?

If you are the owner or manager of your company, it's *up to you* to create the systems that your sales people will use. It's *up to them* to use those systems to close more jobs. You have to simplify the buying process for your team and for yourself. Fewer options will sell better, as do package deals.

———— EXERCISE ————

Take a minute and write down ways you can package your products and programs. How can you make it easier for your customers to buy?

_____

_____

_____

_____

_____

_____

_____

_____

_____

_____

_____

_____

_____

_____

Right Now: Take one product or service and create a good system for your team. Record your progress.

_____

_____

_____

_____

_____

_____

_____

_____

_____

_____

_____

_____

_____

_____

—— WHAT I'VE LEARNED ——

2

GET THE MOST MONEY FOR YOUR PRODUCTS AND SERVICES

Pricing Strategies

"Price is More Important Than Ever Before"

I've been hearing this ridiculous quote as long as I have been in business. Either, there is less business out there to be had so people feel the only way to compete is by being cheaper, or there is a ton of business out there and a ton of competition to go along with it so it's more important now to be cheaper.

My challenge to you is this: If you truly believe price is the most important factor than why are you doing what you do? Why not sell something that's cheaper, like toilets, or soap, or hot dogs? Why are you an interior designer, a plumber, an electrician?

Are you Good at what you do?

Do you provide Great service?

Do you care about your customers?

Do you take Pride in your business and your name?

Do you have specialized knowledge?

How many Years have you been in Your industry?

DO YOU VALUE YOURSELF?

It all comes down to that one question, *"Do You Value Yourself?"* If you don't value what you have to offer, your experience, knowledge, and expertise than why would your customer? If you don't care about how the job is done and you just want to make the sale, then you're just selling a commodity based on price.

But Jerry, I Don't Want To Rip Anyone Off.

What is a "rip off?" When someone gets ripped off it's almost never about the price. The only way you can truly rip someone off is when you don't provide the products and services the customer is paying for. More people are ripped off by companies that charge lower prices, than they ever are by companies that charge higher prices.

Think about that. If you are out there selling roofing and you have the best price in town, you may close every job, but can you afford all the material, the labor, and the mistakes? The cheap guys are always scrambling. They are trying to sell the next job so they can pay for the supplies for the job they sold a week ago.

But I'll Make It Up In Volume

No You Won't! You are not Wal-Mart, you do not have 100s of employees where you can work off a 5 percent profit margin. You may be Two Guys and a Truck, or a company of 10 or 20. You are limited by the clock. Unless you are a one-man show selling stuff on the Internet, your pay is determined by the amount of work your company gets done.

RAISING YOUR PRICES

Did you know you can raise your prices by 10 percent and you would have to lose 40 percent of your business just to break even? *(I'm sure he wasn't the first to say it but I did learn this from Joe Polish so he gets the credit)*

Let's keep this simple. Say you own a barber shop. For a man to get a haircut the price is $20 and you usually see about 250 customers a month.

Total business for the month would be $5000.

Now let's bump that up just 10 percent, so now your total sales would be $5,500. You made an extra $500 and that was all profit. It didn't cost you one dime more to produce an extra $500 per month or $6,000 per year in profits.

One of three things are going to happen when you raise your prices:

1. You will get less business. Some people may get upset and go somewhere else, but usually it's not even 10 percent.

2. You will get about the same amount of business.

3. You will get more business because people value what you do more. You will get a better quality clientele. Your customers will trust you more than they trust the cheap guys. You will make more money; which is what happened to me every time I raised my prices.

WALK THE TALK

I don't just preach these systems I practice them. In the Phoenix market some yutz started selling shutters for $15.95 per foot. This was going on when our price was $21.95 per foot. Instead of reacting to this ongoing trend of building and selling cheaper products, we raised our prices. Four years later they are still selling shutters for $15.95 per foot, not only them, but many others joined in this race to the bottom. Now during this time we've managed to raise our prices and we are $30 per foot for wood shutters, without apologies. We do a fantastic job using top-quality materials and we give our customers the finest service in the valley. Our customers value what we do and proudly refer us to their family and friends. No one has ever complained that we overcharged them.

You might say, *"Yeah, but Jerry, the other product was poor quality, made in China"* or, *"It was built in someone's garage"* and you would be right. But when these cheaper companies go out to a customer's home they say their product is great quality and comes with a lifetime warranty. If they are a trustworthy, likeable salesperson, why wouldn't someone buy from them and save thousands of dollars? Now don't get me wrong, these companies take plenty of market share and I know for a fact that they are busy. In fact they are busier than I ever care to be. They work harder and harder to make less money. As material costs go up they are stuck being the cheap guys. They'll never believe that people will pay more, so they will always be stuck selling cheap products that require warranty work.

Meanwhile our sales are up each year. Our competitors see me at shows and say, "We love going up against you." Instead of wondering how we are doing they are gleeful at getting more business for less profit. Maybe we didn't sell as many shutters as our competition, but our profits are up as is our referrals and reputation with our customers.

SO, ARE YOU WORKING FOR BUSINESS OR FOR PROFITS?

You owe it to yourself, your family, and your customers to be more profitable. That's right you owe it to your customers. Wouldn't it be better to be a reliable company who is in business when their customer has problems? Wouldn't it be better to pay your suppliers on time? Wouldn't it be better to give your employees healthy living wages and some bonuses once in a while, rather than yell and scream about not being able to make payroll? Yes, it's true that money can't buy happiness, but it can buy a boat; and I've never been happier than I am taking my kids out to the lake on a summer afternoon.

IS YOUR CUSTOMER'S BUYING CRITERIA PRICE?

Do you know what your customer's buying criteria is? I hear salesperson after salesperson talk about the price of the product before their client even brings it up as a concern. What if you're selling a refrigerator? Yes it's true people will shop for the best deal, but not always. You happen to offer next day delivery and no hassle hook up. Sure, they can save $100 by going down the road, but they like you and trust you and believe they will get what they want rather than shopping all over town in 110 degree heat just to save a few bucks.

The other big mistake most salespeople make is they can't afford what they are selling so they believe what they are selling is expensive to their customer. Let your customer decide what is expensive and what a great value is. Have you ever tried to sell the same product to two different people? One can't believe what a great deal it is, and the other can't leave your store fast enough. Same products, same prices, two different customers, and two completely different reactions.

DO YOU ASK YOUR PROSPECT WHAT THEIR BUDGET IS?

Although this is a legitimate and common question that sales-people ask, I've never been a fan of the budget question. Most people either don't have an idea of what the project will cost or they are usually guessing on the low side. Most people also don't like to be pigeon-holed into you showing them products that only fit in their budget. How many times did you spend more than you intended because the better option was what you REALLY wanted?

You want to show your customers the highest price product that will fit their needs the best. There are two reasons you should practice top-down selling.

1. You never know what that customer can really afford or what the customer is willing to spend a lot of money on.

2. *(the best reason)* You can have higher margins on your cheaper products. The customer will save money and you will maintain very high profits.

Let me say again, I believe in operating very ethically. I have never had a complaint that I ripped someone off. Give your customer the best service you can, and charge accordingly.

DISCOUNT STRATEGIES

"We have great discounts on all marked up items."

That's the saying I use when customer questions the discounts or sales. They usually laugh and the feeling is, OK This guy's not B-S-ing me.

Discounts, sales, and specials are always a good thing. People love saving money. If you raise your prices it will give you more flexibility to offer greater discounts and savings to your customers.

I used to sell these do-it-yourself styrofoam cornice kits at the home shows. When I got the product from my supplier I thought they were great. It's something that anyone can decorate themselves and you don't even have to know how to sew or upholster. *(Cornices are products that sit above your blinds and help decorate your house.)* We had four styles and two sizes within each style. I had a sheet with all the pricing on it and we proudly displayed them and demonstrated how to decorate them at the show.

We totally bombed! No one purchased a cornice. They all loved them, took the information, and promised to call us back. *I heard that enough in high school to know they wouldn't call back.*

Now when we first got the product I asked the supplier, "How do you sell these?" And they said, "Anyway you want" which is code for, "I have no idea." Well, after that show I decided we would scrap three of the styles. We were only going to sell one style at the home show. I raised my prices significantly and offered a 30 percent discount that was only good at the home show.

We sold $17,000 worth of cornices at that show. We were running back and forth to the warehouse to get more product all weekend long. It was awesome! We also invited all the people who purchased to a decorating seminar the following weekend where we ended up selling another $11,000 worth of cornices to the same people who bought at the show.

Do you see why we had such great success with this system? Notice it had nothing to do with the product. The same product for the same prices would not sell the first time around.

We made it easy for people to buy. They only had one choice instead of four. They didn't know we had three other styles, they gladly purchase the product that was available to them now.

We raised our prices in order to give them a discount. Our final price was higher than the original prices we had.

We had a deadline. They had to buy at the show in order to get the discount. If they purchased at the show we promised to hold the discount for them.

We also had a follow up decorating seminar which was free if you purchased a cornice at the show. We gave out so many tickets that we had to have 2 classes and we ended up having to deliver product because we ran out.

Question: *Which is better, a Dollar Discount or a Percentage Discount?*

Answer: *Test.*

Everyone in my industry offers a percentage off month after month and that's fine but a percentage of what? We tested with a large dollar amount off of a large purchase and people responded really well to that.

One thing I do like about a dollar amount is it's specific. The customer knows how much she is saving, which is important to her. It's funny that when your wife comes home from shopping what does she tell you? *"Honey I saved $500 today."* She never tells you what she spent. That's why on your grocery receipts they make a big deal about how much you SAVED!

Still you want to test different offers and find the formula that people respond to the most. One sale I liked was from The Room Store where they said if you buy $2500 worth of furniture they will give you $500 more for Free. It's great that instead of giving a discount they sold more stuff.

> *"The Impression of a great deal is often times better than a great deal."*
> ~ Jerry Levinson

I noticed places like Kohl's have specials like buy one, get one at 50 percent off. Now, you may have gone in there for one belt or one pair of shoes, but honestly who's not going to get the second item for half off. Of course you can go across the street to Wal-Mart and get two for the same price as one item at Kohl's, but Kohl's is leaving you with a great impression of a great deal!

The fastest way for you to start making more money is for you to raise your prices.

——— EXERCISE ———

Come up with three pricing strategies you can change in your business today to start making more money.

Can you package products together? Can you simply raise your prices 10 - 20 - 30 percent or more? The other advantage of increasing your prices is that you can do small jobs for no discount and you will make more money. You can give someone a better price when they are buying more widgets from you.

Write down your 3 strategies below.

1. _____

_____

_____

_____

_____

_____

2. _____

_____

_____

_____

_____

_____

3. _____

_____

_____

_____

_____

_____

——— WHAT I'VE LEARNED ———

3

CLOSE
MORE SALES

Sales Strategies

In this chapter I will give you several examples of how to sell. Dan Kennedy invented the phrase, *"But I'm in the _____ business, this doesn't apply to my industry."* It doesn't matter what business you are in. All of us have a product or service to sell to a person. These techniques can be applied to any business so don't get caught up in the sample businesses used.

BUILDING RAPPORT

One of the most important parts of the sales process is building rapport.

- *When is the best time to start building rapport?*
- *Is it when your client calls for an appointment?*
- *Is it the first thing you do when you meet your client?*
- *Should you get down to business right away and then build rapport as the appointment goes forward?*

Most books I've read on sales teach that you need to start building rapport first to get to know your client better, and to start building a relationship right away. I don't agree with this.

Building rapport is about getting to know your client on more of a personal level. If you plan on building rapport at a certain point in the sales process it won't come naturally. Your client might feel this is a tactic you are using and they will be annoyed rather than feel appreciated.

When you first show up for an appointment, or when your customer first comes into your showroom, that meeting is happening for a specific reason, there's a specific need the customer has. If you launch into a personal conversation first, it will not be an effective way to begin your relationship. It's better to start off by addressing the reason for their visit.

THE ABSOLUTE BEST TIME TO BUILD RAPPORT

... is when it comes naturally. It happens during the interview process, mostly when you are asking questions about how to best serve your client. Little things slip out, such as kids, relationships, vacations, summer homes, work, sports, etc. Building rapport may be one of the most crucial elements to getting the sale. It's very important, but let it happen naturally.

Some Rules about Building Rapport:

- **Rule #1:** This is about them not you. What is your client's favorite subject to talk about? It's the client. You should discuss things that are interesting to your client.

- **Rule #2:** "Never talk about politics or religion." *How silly.* Of course you talk about politics when you go into someone's home and they have CNN or Fox News on. Especially if you agree with their politics. You may find the customer will buy from you simply because you agree with them on the issues. I've sold many jobs where we started chating about politics. Now, don't fake that you are something you are not.

I find the best way to approach politics is to ask your client, "What do you think about (subject). Let's say there is a debate on gun control. *"What do you think about them trying to pass legislation on more gun control?"* You may find that if you don't agree you will have to keep your mouth shut or just pretend that you don't know much about the issue, but don't lie.

As far as religion goes, there is hardly anything better that you can talk about if you see your client is very religious. Again, you don't have to be very religious but if you take an interest in what is interesting to your client, your client will enjoy your company and will trust you.

If I go to a client's home and they are clearly Jewish you bet I'm going to discuss that with them. Their decision to buy from me may just come down to the fact that they would rather support a fellow Jew than someone else.

When you discuss something your client is interested in, that's when they'll enjoy your visit or conversation the most.

- **Rule #3:** Be observant. If your client is wearing clothes that say he/she supports Michigan State, then talk about that. You don't have to know about everything in order to ask questions and learn what your client is interested in.

If you go to the home for an appointment, do you look at family photos on the wall? If I see photos of people dressed in uniform I'm going to ask them about that. I'm going to mention my son is serving in Afghanistan. If I see a family photo you bet I'm going to ask about their family. I'll mention my adopted kids.

- **Rule #4:** Enjoy your customer, enjoy your job, and enjoy your life. I don't really care what product you are selling, you are doing a great service to your customer, aren't you? One of the largest keys to success is to do something you love doing. When you get the opportunity to work with other people it should be fun.

I've met some great people in my business. I've made many friends. There are customers who will brag about the service we gave them. There are people who are flat out routing for us to succeed. It's just a great feeling to know people out there who keep an eye out for you and who want you and your family to be well.

Love your customers and they will give you all that love right back!

WHAT IS THE BEST WAY TO SELL?

Years ago "The Greatest Sales Trainer Who Ever Lived," Fred Herman, was a guest on *The Tonight Show* with Johnny Carson. Johnny Carson challenged Fred, *"You're the greatest salesman in the world; Sell me something."*

Herman asked, *"What would you like me to sell you?"*

"I don't know," Johnny replied. *"How about this ashtray?"*

"Why the ashtray, Johnny? What is it that you like about that ashtray?" asked Herman.

Carson listed the things he liked: It matched the brown color of his desk, was octagonal and fulfilled the need for someplace to put his ashes.

Then the Herman asked, *"How much would you be willing to spend for a brown octagonal ashtray like that one?"*

"Maybe $20," said Johnny.

"Sold!" said Herman.

One of my favorite new shows is *Car Lot Rescue*. When sales people are asked to give an example of how they sell a car they often reply by saying, "This is a great car. It has leather seats, 6-disc CD, GPS system, automatic windows..." they tell all about the great features and benefits the car has. They only leave out one part.

They didn't ask any QUESTIONS

As Herman did with the ashtray, you can do with any product that you are selling. Ask questions. *Why are you looking for a new car? Is this car going to be used mostly for work? Is good gas mileage important to you? Do you have kids? Do you need to pull a boat or trailer? What color do you like? Do you prefer leather interior or cloth seats? What are some of the features in a car that you are looking for? Would you like to finance the vehicle or are you looking to pay for it in full?*

IT IS BETTER TO UNDERSTAND THAN IT IS TO BE UNDERSTOOD?

This is the greatest lesson I've ever learned about selling and marketing. If you understand what your customer's wants, needs, and desires are, you will be able to provide the best products and services to them.

Selling is really so much easier than we make it out to be. A good salesperson is one who will ask a lot of questions, listen to their customer, listen to their customer, listen to their customer, *(no that's not an error in editing)* and restate what it is that was important to that customer. Customers want to know that you are paying attention to them. They want to feel understood and listened to.

IS IT IMPORTANT TO BE THE EXPERT IN YOUR INDUSTRY?

It's great to be a knowledgeable expert in your industry but it's not the most important thing. It's nice to be able to answer all of your customer's questions and concerns. It's important to learn as much as you can about the products and/or services you provide, but being an expert doesn't make you a great sales person.

Case In Point: The world's worst salespeople: Website developers and search engine optimization guys. *If you happen to be one and you are reading this I hope you find it insulting and you try to understand.*

WE ARE NOT INTERESTED IN HOW SMART YOU ARE!!!

WE WANT CUSTOMERS

Example: You are building and optimizing a website for a landscaper. Most web heads will want to educate their client about how Google works, or how pay-per-click works. You want to tell them about key words, spiders, bounce rates, and little green men who drive traffic to their site.

{Insert rolling eyes here.}

At this point your prospect is rolling his eyes saying, *"Please kill me now."* He is a professional landscaper. He understands what plants and grass grow best in the area. He knows how to mow and maintain a lawn better than anyone and he wants badly to do that for people without learning about internet spiders.

Here's how you sell a Landscaper Web Optimization:

"So, Dave how long have you been a landscaper?"

"Have you been in Phoenix the whole time or did you come from somewhere else?"

"What made you decide to get into the landscape business?"

"Would you prefer to do maintenance or do you want to do full landscaping projects?"

"Who is your best customer? Male or female? Age demographic? Married or single? Do they have kids at home or are they empty nesters?"

"What home values would you like to work on?"

"What area of town would you like to stay in?"

This is a great example of how to build rapport by asking questions that are interesting to your client; and you are finding out your client's exact needs, wants, and desires in regards to building that client's business.

As a Web-Head, you want to get your client the best customers. You don't need to explain every detail about how. If you take an interest in your client and understand what that client is trying to achieve, then the client will trust you and do business with you.

WHY? – WHY? – WHY? – WHY? – WHY?

Why does your customer need your product or service right now? What is the real reason your customer looked you up on-line, called you or stopped into your business?

- Automotive – *Something is wrong with my car It needs to be repaired.*

- Beautician – *I saw a look in a magazine that I want.*

- Plumber – *I have a leaky faucet.*

- Roofer – *There is a leak in my roof. There is also a few loose tiles.*

- Window Coverings – *The old blinds are broken or I don't like the way they look.*

- Flooring – *This carpet has been in the house since it was built. It's holding up fine but I don't like the color.*

The sale is more about "the why"' than it is about the product or solution. Problems sell. Without a problem there is no need for your service, right?

THE BEST SALES TOOL EVER

I got this idea from Joe Polish. The idea was to create a consumer guide. For window coverings, there are a ton of options and each blind covers a certain need. *(A-HA! It's not about the solution, it's about the problem.)* In creating this guide I had to do some research in my brain and on the web. The question I had to answer was, *"What are the most common questions that my customers have been asking me for the past 17 years?"*

Coming up with those questions was more difficult than I thought, but once I did, it made building my consumer guide a piece of cake. So I created "A Consumer Guide for Buying Window Coverings in Arizona." Your consumer guide may be valuable information for the entire planet, but as you will learn in the next chapter, it's best to choose a target niche. The more it's about your customer, the more receptive they will be to the information.

A GUIDE TO PURCHASING WINDOW COVERINGS IN ARIZONA

Most Frequently Asked Questions

I Don't Know What I Want. Where Do I Begin?	1
Should I Use The Same Window Covering Throughout My House?	1
I Hate Verticals!! What Else Is There For My Sliding Glass Door?	2
My Utility Bills Are Soooo High!! Which Type Of Window Covering Will Give Me The Best Insulation?	3
My Husband Works In The Evening. Do You Have Something To Keep Our Bedroom Dark When We Need It?	3
We Have A Golf Course Lot Or A Great View. What Do You Have That Won't Take Away From Our View?	3
I Have Some Funky Windows, Odd Shapes, Arches, Or Really Large Windows. What Are My Options?	4
Are Window Coverings That Lower From The Top A Good Idea? (Top Down-Bottom Up)	5
There's So Much Dust Out Here! Do You Have A Good Low Maintenance Shade Or Something Easy To Clean?	5
What's The Truth About Fake Wood Vs Real Wood Blinds And Shutters?	7
What's New In Window Coverings? Show Me Something I Haven't Seen Before!	7
If I Have Good Blinds Or Shades Now Can I Get Them Repaired?	8
Recommendations For Each Room	8

Here's a sample of what our Consumer Guide looks like.

I want you to notice some things about this guide:

I put the questions right on the front. I can't tell you how many times a customer has read the question and said, *"That's me, I hate verticals,"* or, *"I just asked you if we should do the same window covering in each room."* See, we are *starting a conversation that is already going on in the customer's mind.* What's really great about that is they hardly ever read the answer. Just by stating the question before asking it, you show that you understand your client, which helps build TRUST.

Notice this is in black and white? The whole guide is in black and white. This is not a brochure. This is meant to educate our customer not sell them. Consumer guides are much better than a brochure. Brochures are tools that are used to sell your prospect. Brochures are usually all about your business. They tell how great you are and how much you care. What brochures don't do is address the most important part of the sale, and that's your customer's wants, needs, and desires.

We don't promote Blind Devotion. I explain in the beginning that I'm the author and I give my information on the back cover, but I don't say how great we are or how terrible our competition is. If you give great content and great information to your customer, who else are they going to use? You are also able to slam other products that you don't like without personally attacking another company. It just ads to your credibility.

TALKING BAD OF ANOTHER COMPANY OR SERVICE

I'm not a big fan of negativity, but there is a time and place for it and there is a way it should be done. Let me give you an example. In our industry there are plastic or faux wood products, shutters and blinds. I've never liked the faux products nor do I want to sell them. They don't hold up nearly as well as quality wood, but that is not what I tell the customer.

WHY: The first thing I'm going to ask is why they want the faux products. It's important to find out why they want what they want before you launch into the reasons why they shouldn't have it.

VALIDATE: You want to validate what they already believe so it doesn't come across as you treating them like they're stupid.

"Yeah, I know Mary. A lot of people recommend the faux shutters saying they hold up better. It's a little frustrating because that's not true. It's not that those other people are lying to you, it's just that they don't have as much experience so they're telling you what they believe to be true."

EDUCATE: Now it's your turn to educate them on what you would recommend. *"We've been in the business for 20 years, and from our experience the faux shutters don't look as good as quality wood once installed. You could experience yellowing and warping. Here are some pictures that show what I am talking about."*

I don't care what industry you are in, I know you deal with others in your profession that sell stuff you wouldn't recommend. You can, and you should, educate your customer but keep in mind that they will get put off if you lecture them or treat them as if they're stupid. It's important to first validate what they believe about the information they have learned on the Internet or from another sales person.

CLOSING THE SALE

"If you believe you have the right product or service for your customer than you have an obligation to close as hard as you can."
~ Chet Holmes

I'm going to trust that you're a good and honest person who will serve your customer the best you can. Quite frankly if you are a dishonest creep you probably won't be capable of reading this book anyway.

The first rule to being a great closer is this, **you must respect and value what you do**. If you don't, why should your customer? Do you respect your product, your service, your knowledge, the time you spend with a client, your experience, yourself? Then I trust you'll always do what is in your customer's best interest.

I don't want to teach you a bunch of techniques that you won't use. I'm not comfortable coming across as a pushy salesperson or using certain techniques on customers.

Here are a few simple ideas that everyone can, and should, use:

- *After you give your customer the price, put your pen down and SHUT UP!* Ok, this is the most basic closing-101 technique out there, but it is amazing how many salespeople haven't learned it, so it bears repeating. The rule is *"whoever talks first loses."* One time my wife and I were in a Lazy Boy furniture store buying some chairs. The saleslady gave us the price. My wife and I were looking at fabrics trying to decide which is the best fabric for us. The saleslady, instead of keeping her mouth shut, got nervous and blurted out, *"Maybe I can get you a better price."* Well, guess what? Now you have to. We ended up leaving because she couldn't give us a better price. Eventually we came back but they had to throw in some throw pillows. Now don't get me wrong here, we weren't working her at all, it was just human nature and the flow of the sale, and she *blew it* by not waiting to talk. If you truly get nervous and can't keep your mouth shut, try asking a question that is not price related. You can simply say, *"So what do you think?"*

- *My favorite closing method is to "Assume the Sale."* *"Ok, the repair on your roof will be $5320, we have one job ahead of you so would it work if we got started on Thursday at 10AM?"* Or, *"This dining room table and chairs is only $950; would Friday or Saturday work better for you for delivery?"* Blinds take two weeks to deliver and install; shutters normally take about five weeks. I teach my salespeople to know the dates going into an appointment and offer to schedule the installation ahead of time. We may have to adjust but the goal is to get the sale and take care of the customer.

The great thing is if you do all the other steps right:

- Building Rapport
- Asking Questions
- Understanding Your Customer's Buying Criteria
- Understanding Your Customer's Needs, Wants, and Desires

... then closing the sale will be the easiest part.

4

FIND YOUR
BEST CUSTOMERS
Marketing Strategies

"You are not in the flooring business or the chiropractic business or the accounting business, you are in the marketing business."
~ Dan Kennedy

This is an amazing revelation when you make it. Most of us get into our business because we enjoy being the expert and professional in our chosen field. We are so good at what we do that it's easy and it becomes natural. It's great to be an excellent technician, but that's not enough to run a great business. In fact, the best marketers will build the greatest businesses.

We opened up a new showroom in 2010 in a fantastic location in a busy strip mall with lots of traffic. The showroom was beautiful. It had the best and largest selection of flooring in Arizona, the best selection of window coverings, beautiful kitchen cabinets, slate countertops and area rugs.

"If You Build It They Will Come"
~ *Field of Dreams*

Well, we built it and guess what? No one came. Who really cares how great your showroom is or how great your location is? There really is only one thing consumer's care about... themselves!

Sure, having a great location that's conveniently located is important. It's important that your showroom isn't cluttered and it looks great. It's important how your employees greet people as they walk in the door. I'm not saying this stuff isn't important, but what I am saying is that if you don't tell people about your showroom it really doesn't matter how great it is.

SOMETHING TO CONSIDER

Quite frankly there are a lot of businesses that do quite well without the overhead and hassle of a showroom. If you can invest $10,000 a month into marketing rather than in a great showroom you'll probably have greater sales than a company that has a fantastic showroom. I personally like having a showroom for my employees and my customers. I like having a place to do business at rather than go to the customer's home for everything. You do attract a higher-end customer with a showroom because it does give you more credibility.

CAUTION: Do not open up a business without a decent marketing budget!

What's a reasonable budget for your advertising? It really depends on what you are selling. It depends on who your customers are, what it takes to reach them, what kind of profit you have, what the "Lifetime Value" of your customers are, etc. At one time I was spending more than 15 percent on advertising. Since I learned about advertising, mainly "Direct Response Advertising," I only spend 8 to 10 percent of our annual sales on advertising.

I have a friend who owned a hearing aid company. His budget for marketing was closer to 30 percent. I have another friend who owns a roofing company and spends only 5 percent on advertising. There really isn't a *right* answer as to what percentage you should spend, but you should know your numbers and you should track your marketing like crazy.

You want to know which advertising will attract the best customers:

- What type of ad will make your phone ring?
- Which ad brings you the highest ticket customers?
- What is your closing rate for each advertisement?
- Which form of media works best?
- Which offer works best?
- What time of year do you get the best results?
- When do you invest more for your advertising?

You want to make sure that every employee is asking the customers where they heard about you. Even if you don't invest in a sophisticated system to track your leads and marketing, you should ask your customer where they heard about you and write it down on an order form. A lot of business people don't track this well enough, and it's this one thing that can make the biggest difference in your success.

Have you ever watched, *Shark Tank*? If you are a business person, *you have to watch this show!* It's a show where entrepreneurs have the opportunity to present their product or service to four high level investors (the Sharks) who may take a risk and invest in their company. Now "the Sharks" are multi-millionaires, so if they invest in your company, they'll do everything in their power to be sure it succeeds (and to protect their egos). BUT—**THEY WILL NOT INVEST IN YOUR COMPANY IF YOU DON'T KNOW YOUR NUMBERS!** *(and be able to regurgitate that information on the spot!)*

It really doesn't matter how cool your product or service is,

I've seen many great ideas get passed up by the Sharks, so you need to know:

- What it costs to make your widget
- How much you can sell it for retail
- How much you can sell it for wholesale
- How much does it cost to acquire a customer!
- What is the lifetime value of the customer

Now, they are also going to ask you what your sales are so far and how much money you've made. The people who get the deals, the people who are the most successful entrepreneurs, *are the ones who know their numbers.* They are the ones who understand their business best and can articulate it in a way that will attract an investor instead of repel one.

WHO'S YOUR COMPETITION?

When you are advertising your product or service, who are you competing against? It may not be who you think. If you are a dentist, a lawyer, a roofer, or a veterinarian, who is your competition when you are marketing?

EVERYONE!

You aren't competing against the people who are in the same industry, you are competing against everyone who is in the Val-Pak with you. When someone opens up a Val-Pak and all those 1/3 page coupons coming falling out, why will someone stop and look at your coupon? When your ad plays on the radio you are competing against other advertisers, the music, and the DJ or talk show host. Why will someone stop and listen to what you have to say? When John decides to read the newspaper, he's looking at it to get the news. How is he going to notice your ad? In this case you are competing against other advertisers as well as the news.

RULE #1 GET NOTICED!

It really doesn't matter how great your product or service is, or how awesome your prices are. If people don't see your ad, if they don't notice what you are selling, then your phone isn't going to ring.

One of the greatest ways you can stand out is by using a *"Killer Headline!"* When writing your headline you want to address a pain point that your client has. *Problems sell!* Be sensational! Get attention!

Here was a heading I saw in a Facebook ad. The person who ran the ad specializes in helping women (between the age of 30 and 45 who are mothers) lose weight.

"See What This Guy Did to My Mother!"

Instead he could have said:

"See What This Guy Did for My Mother!"

Let me ask you a question: *Which headline gets your heart pumping? Which ad sounds like an interesting story vs a solicitation?* Notice how different these two ads are just by changing one word; "to" to "for."

Here's an ad for security doors from a coupon-type magazine. The heading is:

Enjoy the Fresh Air While Increasing Security and Adding Home Value!

OK, he's stating some benefits. It's obviously a solicitation, and it's a little weak.

How about:

13 Homes Were Broken Into in Sun Lakes Since January 2013!

If I lived in Sun Lakes I would be interested in hearing about that. After that heading you'll think about how it could be prevented by adding a security door. You can also explain the additional benefits you'll get from owning a security door and include customer's testimonials.

You never want to use your company name as the heading. Remember when you are advertising, it's about the customer, not about you. Your goal is to get your prospect's attention and to get them to call you. The name of your company, phone number, address, and website can be placed at the bottom

Here's another example from a remodeling company:

Headline: Remodeling Made Affordable

Sub-head: We Do It All – No Job is Too Small

This headline is wrong on so many levels. First of all, it's a price headline. They are basically saying we want any cheap pathetic job because we like doing remodeling projects and we are cheap. Remodeling what? Kitchens, bathrooms, family rooms? *They do it all*, the problem is customers are usually not looking for everything.

How about this for a heading:

Special Report Reveals Why 7 Out of 10 Kitchen Remodeling Projects Take Too Long and Go WAY Over Budget!

That's sensational! Even if you're not ready to remodel your kitchen you want to read this special report because—let's face it—everyone loves a train wreck.

Here are several headlines you can use, or change, for your industry.

Dan Kennedy calls it "Swipe and Deploy." The idea is to take great ideas from other industries and use it in your own industry.

- Carpet Cleaner: *Special Report Reveals 7 Things You Should Know Before Getting Your Carpets Cleaned*

- Carpet Sales: *Consumer Alert! Get Your Free Consumer Guide Explaining the 13 Things You Should Know Before Purchasing Carpet in Seattle*

- Weight Loss: *Why 7 Out of 10 Men Over 40 Fail to Lose Weight or Keep the Weight Off!*

- Exterminator: *3 Free Ways to Keep Your House Pest Free This Summer!*

- Garage Floor Epoxy: *The Greatest Cure for Dingy, Dirty, Grimy, Greasy, Disgusting, Oily Garage Floors!*

- Water Softeners: *City Announces a Major Contamination in Water! Find Out How to Keep Your Family Safe!*

- Garage Storage: *Are You Tired of All the CLUTTER in Your House? Are You Embarrassed to Invite Your Family or Friends Over?*

- Restaurant: *Food Fight! Who's Going to Win? YOU DECIDE.* (Here you can have a picture of a cow fighting a chicken.)

- Furniture Store: *Discover the 7 Most Important Factors You Should Know Before Buying New Furniture!*

- Remodeler: *Have Your Dream Kitchen in Just 20 Days!*

- Pool Builder: *Pool Builder Reveals the 18 Most Important Things to Consider Before Building Your Dream Pool*

- Carpet Store: *Allergy Suffers Discover Why Carpet is the Best Flooring Solution After All*

- Chiropractor: *Headaches and Migraines Cured Without Harmful Drugs. Find Out How!*

Now it's your turn. Use the next page to come up with seven eye-catching headlines. Use words that create raw emotion. Dan Kennedy teaches, the best place to study and look at headlines is *The National Enquirer.* Do you realize how often you notice *The National Enquirer* on news stands at checkout counters? That's because they do a fantastic job writing sensational headlines. In fact they are so sensational you are standing between the magazine and your kid so she doesn't see that Madonna is now sleeping with three men and two of them are gay. It doesn't matter that little Sallie is only four and can't quite read. As a business person and marketer, you should check out the headlines even if you're embarrassed by the content. Look up magazines online and come up with your own emotionally-driven, eye-catching, sensational headlines.

———— EXERCISE ————

Write your seven eye-catching headlines:

1. _____

_____

2. _____

_____

3. _____

_____

4. _____

_____

5. _____

_____

6. _____

_____

7. _____

_____

RULE #2 SELECT A TARGET AUIDENCE

(This is so important it's often Rule #1 for most marketers.)

Joe Polish and Dean Jackson are two of the best marketers on the planet. They have created "The 8 Profit Activators."

The first is, *Choose Your Target Audience.*

So who is your target audience? Who is the best customer you have? Who's going to spend the most money with you? Who is going to refer their friends and family to you?

Selecting a target audience is the greatest way to get the best results from your advertising. I know your product or service can help a multitude of people, but the best way to get results is too narrowly focus on who is your best customer.

This is not to the exclusion of others.

Choosing a target audience does not mean you can't serve other customers. It just means that you choose who your best customers are. Whenever I join a networking group there is always a chiropractor in there who will say, *"We can help anyone with a spine."* OK, that's cute, but who is he talking about? Who comes to mind when the chiropractor is looking for people with a spine? I know another chiropractor who specializes in helping female golfers between the ages of 50 and 65. Do you know any women golfers who are between the ages of 50 and 65? I bet you are trying to think of someone right now, or this may even be you. If it is, aren't you curious what this chiropractor does that specifically helps women golfers?

There is a financial advisor named Mary in Sun City, AZ, who has her niche down so well she only attracts the best clients who will trust her and stay with her for life.

She's looking for:

- Married couples between the ages of 55 and 65.
- They have never been divorced, so they have been married a long time.

- They have kids who are grown and out of the house.
- They are active; they go on vacations or enjoy tennis, golf or some other activity.
- They are Conservative in their politics.
- They chose to live in Arizona. They have the means to move elsewhere but they like it here.

Now Mary happens to have a lot in common with her ideal client, and when she introduces herself in her advertising she explains:

"I've been married to my husband John for 22 years."

"We have two kids, one is married, and the other is going to college."

"We love Arizona and the Southwest."

"John and I love camping up in Sedona."

Do you see where this is going? Mary is making a much bigger connection to her ideal client then she would if she were to say, "I've been a financial advisor for 13 years and I have a portfolio worth 32 million dollars, yada, yada, yada. The same stuff that most financial advisors say.

Mary has built trust with her ideal client. In fact building trust was easy for Mary. The challenge for Mary was figuring out who exactly is her best client. When you figure out whom your ideal client is, your marketing will become much easier. You will build trust and loyalty with your ideal client and you will profit greater from your ideal client.

Now build an avatar of what the perfect customer looks like to you. *Who has been your best customer? Who do you want to be a "Hero" to?*

- Are they male or female?
- What is their age bracket?

- Are they married or single? Divorced or widowed?
- What is their education?
- Do they have kids?
- Are they empty nesters?
- Do they live in multiple homes?
- What are their religious beliefs? Political preferences?
- What are their hobbies?

You can have more than one avatar—more than one target market—but the key to successful marketing is to advertise

"One product to one person at one time."
~ Chet Holmes

ONE PERSON

When you are advertising, whatever your message is has more to do with who you're advertising to than the product or service you are providing. If you want to capture your *best prospects attention* your ad should be about that prospect.

Examples:

"We have the perfect workout for men between the age of 40 and 55 who are busy executives who need more energy, and who don't have much time."

If you meet this description than you are probably curious what the workout is about. Notice that you don't even have to talk about the workout plan. All you have to do is describe the perfect customer.

My sister is 37 years old and she is so busy driving her kids back and forth to school, she doesn't have time to work out, and she's very frustrated dieting while the rest of her family eats anything they want. Not to mention she has to cook the food for them that she can't even enjoy. She has a stack of clothes in her closet that she hasn't thrown out because she is determined to fit into them again someday. The problem is, she only has about 30 minutes a day to herself.

The biggest achievement you can have in any ad is to:

"Start a conversation that is already going on in your prospects mind"

If you can do this, your prospective customer will trust you, will like you, and will buy whatever you are selling because you understand her. Just as in sales, when you are marketing to your client it is:

"Better to understand then it is to be understood."

I know I've repeated these quotes a couple times in this book, but these two quotes are the most important statements to remember when it comes to sales and marketing. When you understand your customer and you can start a conversation that is already going on in that customer's mind, there will be no limit to the success you can achieve. The sooner you understand that what you do is about the customer and not you, the quicker you will reach your goals.

If you are a loan officer, the number of years you have been in business and the awesome branch where you work is not important to a business owner. What's important to him is that you understand the frustrations he is going thru trying to make payroll, waiting on his customers to pay, the non-sense and bureaucracy of trying to get a simple loan, the time it will take to fund the loan, and all the pain, stress, and worry that he's going thru right now.

If you are advertising for your flooring store, don't tell a customer how big your showroom is or how big the selection is or how great you are. I've always had a rule when designing ads. **NEVER** offer great quality, service, or price in your advertisement. Customers expect that anyway and it's not impressive to see it in an ad. Quite frankly, it's a waste of marketing real estate.

What does your customer want when getting new flooring? It's probably to get the carpet installed fast. The customer probably wants to know that you're going to take great care of the furniture. You can tell the customer that you have a Consumer Guide explaining the seven things that should be considered before buying carpet in Arizona. You can tell the customer about the excellent stain guard you have in case she has a dog who she loves more than her husband. This carpet is easy to clean and we give a complimentary professional cleaning for 12 months. *What can you offer your prospect that is important?*

Our customer is Suzie. She lives in a 2,500 sq. ft. house in a retirement community in Arizona. She doesn't have kids but she does babysit her granddaughter for her son. She also enjoys golf and she wouldn't dream of leaving her clubs in the garage. Suzie's husband Gary likes to work in the garage building doll houses which he sells on the Internet. He's a retired engineer from Intel, but lucky for you, he doesn't care about the kind of carpet his wife chooses. The house is Suzie's and it's her decision.

Suzie is also a clean freak who made you take off your shoes before measuring her old carpets, even though they are dirty and in need of replacement. She likes a clean house but she will also keep her doors and windows open for fresh air, which you know will bring in dust and dirt. Suzie's home is contemporary now, but she is planning on repainting and is also going to replace her furniture. Susie hates it when you see foot prints on the carpet as well as dents from the furniture.

Can you see how knowing and understanding Suzie is more important than knowing and understanding carpets? This will help you:

1. Understand her
2. Build rapport

3. Sell to her

4. Follow up with her

5. Get referrals from her

6. Market to her

REMEMBER: When you are advertising, promoting, selling, or servicing your client, it's about them, not you!

ONE PRODUCT

I see ads all the time with a menu of all the stuff a company provides. When you ask the owner about their ads they say, "I want to tell them everything I do."

"When you try to Sell everyone everything you will end up selling no one anything."

As a consumer we look for very specific things.

- "I need tires for my Toyota Tundra truck" not I need something for my car.

- "I need Dog food for my Sharpe" not food for my pet.

- "I need a nice suit for a wedding," not clothing.

- "I need carpet for my home," not I need flooring.

- "I want wood shutters for my arched windows," instead of I need window coverings.

Have you ever looked at signs as you were driving down the road to see what they said? Let's say you are on your way to Home Depot shopping for new carpeting. You probably passed two flooring stores on the way where you could have looked at new carpet for your home. The problem is most companies advertise flooring instead of carpet. Now their logic is, *"We sell tile, hardwood, laminate, vinyl, and carpet. We can't just advertise carpet."*

What they should do is advertise carpet and get as many

people in their showroom as they can. Once the prospect is in the showroom it's the salesperson's responsibility to make sure that customer knows everything they do. You job is to make the phone ring or get the customer in your showroom so you can educate her of all the services you provide.

We all have a *reticular activating system* in our brain that helps us see and attract what we want. It's like when you're looking to buy a car. Have you noticed it seems like a lot of people own that same vehicle? If you want to buy a red Ford Mustang you will start seeing red Mustangs all over the road. If you want a blue Toyota Tundra pickup truck you will start seeing blue Toyota Tundra trucks everywhere. How come you didn't notice them before? It's because you are now in tune to the object you desire most, so you will start to see it everywhere. You will start to see TV commercials and hear radio ads, you'll see newspaper ads for the product you now want.

It's the same with any product or service your customer is looking for. If you do some research as to the most popular Google search terms for your business, you're going to find the most basic terms are used more often than the professional definition of what you do. If you are a chiropractor, are you providing chiropractic care or do you offer pain relief? *What is your customer looking for?* If you are an excellent remodeler who is capable of building a house from the ground up, you will attract more customers by offering kitchen remodeling than by offering to do anything they need. *What is your best client typing into a Google search to find you?*

Note: Don't confuse what I am saying here with Internet advertising. The popular search terms you find in Internet advertising are the same terms that will work best in print advertising, radio, or TV.

I also hated the term "contractor." Sure a painter is a contractor but does anyone type contractor into Google search terms to find a painter? Of course not. If the brakes are bad in your car are you going to look for an auto mechanic or are you going to do a search on brakes? If your air conditioning is on the fritz are you looking for an HVAC repair company or are you looking for an air conditioning company?

When you are advertising your products or service keep the most basic, simple-to-understand terms your prospect is seeking. Check out this example:

> When I type in, "the thing that makes my garage door open" I get 96,000,000 results on Google vs garage door spring which gets 44,300,000 results on Google.

See the difference between talking like your prospects and talking like a garage door repairman—professional. There are twice as many results for the phrase, "the thing that makes my garage door open."

Sorry I got a little off track on this subject, which is about marketing one product or service at a time. This also goes back to what I wrote about in Chapter 1, *Making the Buying Process Easier.*

That's exactly what we are doing by marketing one product. We want to make it easy for our customer to find what they are looking for and come after it. Don't make them guess at what you do. Don't make it difficult for them to find what it is that they are looking for.

AT ONE TIME

> *Who are the best sellers of products, goods, and services?*

QVC and Groupon.

> *Why?*

Is it because you can get products cheaper thru these sources?

NO

Is it because of the outstanding quality these companies sell?

NO

Do they have the best most expensive marketing systems?

NO, not really

Then why is it these two companies sell millions of dollars' worth of merchandise every year?

Because the clock is ticking!

Both these companies put a time limit on how long you have to make a decision. Knowing that the clock is ticking you are more likely to buy because of your limited opportunity to own the product at the specially announced price. Here's the dirty little secret: *many times the price isn't really marked down.* They are masters at giving you the perception of value.

If you limit the quantity of people who can take advantage of your special offer, people will feel more anxious to take advantage and save money or get the "freebie." Let's say you do bathroom remodels and the first seven who sign up with you will get a brand new sink, FREE *($395 Value)*. Create a little scarcity and see if you can increase your response rate. So what if you end up with 10 customers? You give away 10 sinks. What do you care? You just created a bigger demand for your service. You can limit the offer in your ad and it's your choice if you want to sell over the limit you set or hold tight to the rules you created.

Notice all the sales on Black Friday that end at 10 a.m.? Why do you think they do that? You have people who can't show up at 8 a.m. to get to work on time, yet they can show up at the shopping mall at 5:30 a.m. so they can beat the limited quantity or the clock. Would they sell just as much merchandise if they didn't create such excitement and risk of losing out? *Probably not.*

Don't get wrapped up in the idea that it's not real because the special offer came out of your head. It will be real to your customers, and your employees. If you can motivate more people to do business with you then you should create as much excitement and buzz around your sale as you can. I don't want you to be dishonest, mislead, or lie, but it's perfectly legitimate to offer a special deal with limited quantities and a limited amount of time.

> *"If two companies are identical, carrying the same products and offering the same service, the one who fascinates will win every time."*
> ~ Sally Hogshead

If you look through the magazines you'll see business people get real lazy about creating offers and excitement. They run the same ad month after month. They may change the heading once in a while, or throw in some holiday graphics, but for the most part their offer is always the same.

I always loved it when our manufacturer had a special that wasn't that good. The people in the window covering industry would gripe and complain and it would absolutely stifle them. Instead of figuring a better offer or a unique special they would only run with the manufacturer's coupon or rebate. It always gave us an edge by being able to offer our customers something different, something more, something unique in the industry.

In fact creativity is dead in advertising with most companies. I pulled together 20 ads for the same product, wood shutters. All 20 ads look alike. They have different information as to who the company is and where you can buy them, but they all have the same kind of photos, the same crappy headline, and the same exact offer. You can put any name in anyone of these ads and no one would know the difference.

For most business owners all they do is look to see what the competition is doing and they follow that lead, figuring, *"Well, if Dan is getting business with this ad it must be working."* Then I ask, *"Why do you think Dan is getting business off this ad?"* The reply is always, *"Well, he wouldn't run the ad if he wasn't getting business off of it."* Yes, he actually would run the ad no matter what the ROI is. The reason he'll keep running an ineffective ad is because Dan has no system for tracking. He's also running the ad because his logic is the same: *"Everyone else is running this same ad so it must be working."* The fact is the people who see your ad the most will be your competition.

If you are a plumber you see and hear every ad for plumbing. You will see billboards, signs, newspaper ads, coupon ads, and you will think to yourself, *"Man is Johnny Rooter doing great! Look at all of his ads."* Don't be fooled into believing that your customers are seeing all the ads you see.

This ad is from a flooring and granite company:

Here's what they did wrong.

1. They are not focused on ONE product in their heading. In fact they are trying to tell everyone everything they do.

2. They are adding to the mix by saying they do shower remodeling. These guys want to tell everyone everything.

3. *"Compare Our Quality Prices and Installation"* Why give anyone any reason to compare you against another company? Is your objective to be the cheapest guys out there or would you like to do an excellent job and be paid well for it?

4. They show a couple prices for projects down below assuming that price is their customer's buying criteria.

5. There is really no call to action in this ad.

6. The photo is very bland with no vibrant colors.

Here's what they could have done better.

1. In one spot they mention a *7-Day Turn Around.* That's something important to people who are remodeling their kitchens. The heading could have been:

   Brand New Kitchen in Just 7 Days! We Guarantee It!

2. The photo should have people in it. People will look at pictures that have people in them. It's easier to see yourself in a photo when you see other people there.

3) This ad should focus on one product. Whichever product is their best-selling product. Then they should have a system where they educate their clients on all the other services they provide.

4) I'm not a believer in advertising price. I think you can offer an outstanding discount and give a date that your sale expires, but you need to ask yourself if the price you are showing is the reason your prospect will call. Has it worked in the past?

This ad is from a garage repair Company:

This ad isn't too bad. It could have been better, and I've seen this ad in a couple of places as well. I like the colors they use. Black and yellow really stand out and look sharp, but the ad has too much info in it.

1. First, I do like the heading they used. It's not the name of the company and they did a good job getting right to the point of their prospects problems.

2. I've looked at many garage door repair ads and I can't figure out why none of them have a broken tweaked out garage. As a photo it would stand out much better than a clean looking garage that doesn't need repair.

3. The rest of this ad is just way too busy. For some reason they put the truck in there. Who Cares?

Here's what I would have done.

1. Keep the heading the same.

2. Change the photo so that it's a broken garage door. It's not like it would be a hard picture to get since they see one every day.

3. He makes the promise that it will be *Fixed Today!* Speed of service is very important in today's society and he should be making a bigger deal about that.

4. I would clean this whole ad up by dropping all the coupon crap on the right that is more detail than anyone needs. All these customers need is the phone number, and the company can answer all their questions.

Ad for garage overhead storage racks:

This is a really good ad. It stands out in a pack of coupons or a magazine because the picture is really compelling. Having four people hanging from the rack is interesting, and even if you weren't in the market for this product you might just stop and look to see what's going on here.

They have smaller photos on the sides which are probably unnecessary. If I were to make any changes to this ad it would be to make the center photo the whole ad and drop the side photos.

Ad for a real estate agent:

Got to love this headline, actually, *you really don't.*

What is the number one thing people want when buying a new home? To be honest I don't know the answer but I guarantee you it's not to save $5,000. I bet you that you can come up with five major concerns people have before investing in a new home. Let's give it a shot.

1. Where is the home located?
2. What is the size of the home?
3. How many bedrooms and bathrooms?
4. Backyard or landscaping?
5. Does it have a pool?
6. Is it move-in ready?
7. Does it have a 2-car or 3-car garage?
8. What is the price range?
9. Can I get financing?

In this ad the realator has several different homes to choose from. He has five listings and four ads. He's trying to be everything to everybody which is a big mistake.

How about this for a heading:

Free Report Reveals the 10 Most Important Things You Should Consider Before Buying a Home In Arizona

Or

Fill Out Our Free Questionnaire to Help You Get the Best Home in The Best Location for You and Your Family

As for the listings, it looks like they have several companies trying to advertise on the same page. This kind of approach seems smart since you are spreading the expense, but in the end it is ineffective and it's a waste of money.

This ad is for an air conditioning company:

For the love of God, I wish people would quit using *BEAT THE HEAT* as a slogan. This ad was placed in August and we've had three months of over 100 degree temperatures, so no one is beating the heat.

1. It looks like they are offering some pretty big rebates. That may have been something good to mention in their headline.

2. I'm not sure why they want a large picture of the technician in the ad.

3. A photo of a technician bent down in front of a unit would have been a better shot.

4. The ad is clean and easy to read but it is also an ad that gets passed up very easy because it's hard to tell what they are selling. You have to make an instant impression when you are competing against other advertisers.

Ad for a new fitness gym:

I got this ad in the mail the other day and if it weren't for the fact that I'm interested in all ads, I would have thrown it in the trash right away. It's too big of a mystery what the ad is about.

The big message is that they are *Coming Soon!* That's great, I'm so excited that this new company is *Coming Soon!* I don't know who they are or what they do but they are going to be here real soon.

One thing I learned from Joe Polish and Dan Kennedy is to never fall in love with your ad. These people are in love with their message and they want to tell everyone about *The Orange Effect.*

They aren't interested in the wants and needs of their customers. It's more important for them to tell people about themselves.

How do we improve this ad?

The first thing we have to do is consider what's important to the customers. I've never owned a gym and, quite frankly, I hate working out so let me take a stab at this.

- Location is important.
- Instructors are important.
- Convenient operating hours
- Their workout equipment
- Classes for aerobics, yoga, spinning, etc.

I bet if they took the time to interview people who work out they can find out a whole lot more about what is important to them. If you find that out build your ad around those things that are important to your prospects.

5

THE BEST WAY TO GROW YOUR BUSINESS

Hiring Great Salespeople

"One of the best ways to grow your business is to hire new sales people."
~ Quote from all business people who have done this

The fastest way to grow your business is to hire new salespeople. It's one of those changes most small business people are reluctant to make. Since most small business owners start out as the technician, or the expert in their field, they have a very difficult time giving over any responsibility to someone who is not as smart as they are. If you are incapable of relinquishing control over every aspect of your business you will never be able to truly grow your business. If you are the only person you can rely on, then anytime you take a vacation, get sick, get injured, or step away, your business STOPS and you don't make any money!

One of the reasons people give for not wanting to hire a new salesperson is the amount of money it would cost them. Let me ask you this, If you had a new salesperson, how much extra money could they bring you in a year? What if you had a total bad ass rock star selling for you? How much would that mean to your business? $100,000? - $500,000? - $1Million or more? If you were to hire someone who could bring you an extra $500,000 a year, how much could you afford to pay that person? This is important because you will build your ad around this.

How much can one additional salesperson sell?

_____

How much can you afford to pay that person if he/she sells that amount? _____

If the best salesperson could add $1,000,000 to your bottom line, could you afford to pay her $100,000?

I'm going to give you strategies you can use to hire, train, and maintain great, productive, hard-working, loyal employees. I'm going to show you:

1. How to place an ad for a new salesperson.

2. How to interview and find the best salesperson, or any employee.

3. How to lay down clear expectations for your new employee.

4. A pay structure you can use to get your salesperson on straight commission.

5. Strategies to get rid of a bad salesperson or employee that is fair and helpful to both you and your employee.

Hiring a salesperson or any position is tough. It doesn't matter that the unemployment rate is high and many people need a job. You don't want to just hire anyone, you want the best. Let's look at some of the reasons why we are reluctant to hire a salesperson.

1. *"They are not going to do as good of a job as me because they won't care as much I do."*

2. *"It's difficult to train new people on my product line."*

3. *"I don't want to train somebody and turn that person into my competition."*

4. *"People are lazy and they won't work for commission only."*

5. *"It's frustrating, I feel like I'm dealing with my kids and yet he's a 55 year old man!"*

6. *"The last person I hired stole from me."*

7. *"My other salesperson treats new people rudely and is worried about competing for leads."*

8. *"I can't afford all the benefits so I can't compete for a good salesperson."*

9. *"I'm worried I won't have enough leads or business to keep a salesperson busy and making money."*

10. *"I hate firing people, in fact I can't. I still have someone working for me that I would love to get rid of."*

These are all legitimate reasons many of us use to avoid hiring a salesperson. *So, how do you overcome the challenges you face in hiring someone new?* The answer is you create systems to hire the best, maintain the best, and to grow your business.

I will show you how to avoid the challenges of hiring and how to find the right person for the job. As I've said in other chapters you have to **RESPECT YOURSELF** first! This means you have to see the value in the position and your company. The person you are hiring is looking for a way to work and feed his/her family. You are providing that opportunity. It's the noblest thing any of us can do, give someone a **JOB**!

With that said, you also have to be a strong leader, and you have to be willing to fire someone. I've heard story after story of people who just could not fire the worst employees. You may have an emotional attachment. That employee may have a wife and kids, or some medical challenges, or they may be related to you, or you may simply get so nervous at the thought of firing another human being that it just makes you ill.

You are the risk taker who gave this person an opportunity. Do not allow someone to wreck what you have worked so hard to build. They will survive without you and you will be happier when you drive up to your business and you don't see his car in the parking lot. It's tough but you have faced more difficult challenges so be tough!

So let's talk about what kind of person you are looking for. It would be great to hire someone with experience. Unfortunately they are really hard to find. Quite frankly you will be better off hiring a great salesperson who you can train than someone who has experience, but may not be as good at closing a sale.

First thing you want to do is be really clear about the position and your expectations. ***Write down all the things you want your new salesperson to do:***

1. Will they be required to get their own leads or will you be providing leads, or a combination of both?

2. If you are requiring them to get their own leads, do you want them to make phone calls, canvas neighborhoods, hold a sign up on the street corner? Be specific as to how you expect them to get their own leads.

3. Will they need to have a reliable vehicle or are you going to provide a company car? (If it's their car, do you want them to put signs on it?)

4. Is there a certain age range that would be most ideal for the position? *(You will have to check the laws in your state about what is discriminatory, but you can still write down who will be the best fit for your company, even if you don't put that in your ad.)*

5. Will they have to have specific computer skills, education, or experience?

6. Will they need to work long hours or weekends or odd times?

7. What kind of attitude do you want them to have? Do they have to be outgoing and dynamic?

You want to have a very clear description of the type of person you are going to hire. Write it down on paper. In fact write it in a note pad and carry it around with you for a week. Every time you meet a waitress or checkout clerk at the grocery store, observe the personality traits they have that attract you and the ones they have that repel you.

Also list things you don't want to have:

1. You probably don't want someone who is married to their cell phone. You would be amazed at the amount of applicants who will check their phone for an e-mail or text message during an interview. Imagine how much they will be on their phone while you are paying them.

2. What if they have visible tattoos or body piercing? Is this something that will repel your customers?

   If you are giving into charity I appreciate that and I applaud you, but now is not the time to hire someone based on them being down on their luck. Trust me you will regret it and you will have an even tougher time trying to let that person go.

——— EXERCISE ———

Use this page to write down all the qualities and skills you are looking for in your new employee:

_____

_____

_____

_____

_____

_____

_____

_____

_____

_____

_____

_____

_____

_____

_____

_____

_____

_____

_____

_____

_____

_____

_____

_____

_____

_____

_____

_____

Use this page to write down all the things you DON'T want in a new employee:

_____

_____

_____

_____

_____

_____

_____

_____

_____

_____

_____

_____

_____

_____

_____

_____

_____

_____

_____

_____

_____

_____

Chet Holmes describes, *"The best salesperson is someone who has a lot of empathy and someone who has a big ego."*

The challenge you face as an employer is this: *empathy is great!* You want to find someone who is good at building rapport, and in most cases salespeople are good at telling you about themselves. The real challenge is recognizing a good salesperson, someone who possesses a healthy, strong ego. We usually don't like them in an interview. They're cocky, arrogant, and we think they won't listen. But these are the people who can close sales, and you better snatch them up fast before they open up across the street and clobber you.

Now, you know the amount you can afford to pay your "Superstar" salesperson. You know what personality traits you are looking for, so let's create an ad.

$70,000 a year for Superstar Salesperson!

(Don't bother responding to this ad unless you think you have what it takes!)

We are looking to hire people who are willing to work hard and do whatever it takes to succeed.

You will be selling high-end flooring to clients in the Scottsdale area.

We will provide you with leads, but you will be expected to join networking groups, call past customers, put a sign on your vehicle, and work our programs to acquire, nurture and develop your own leads

Young or old, it doesn't matter. We can tell if you have the right stuff.

You must not be married to your cell phone and no visible tattoos are allowed.

We don't hire based on resumes.

Call for a quick phone interview to see if you qualify to come in for an interview.

I learned a lot of this is stuff from Chet Holmes and applied it to my own business. When your applicant calls for an interview you want to put them on the spot right away.

"Hi Mary, Thanks for calling, why don't you tell me why you think you're a top salesperson?"

See how they perform under pressure. Can they even answer that question? This is more about how your customers may treat your salesperson, depending on the type of sales you are doing. You may want to be tough on this applicant to see if they can work their way into an interview; or if it's a decorator or a position that requires more empathy and less ego, you might go a little easier on this applicant. You can save yourself a whole lot of time just by doing a simple 30-second phone interview.

If the applicant qualifies to come in for an interview, ask her to submit a form explaining the five reasons she believes you should hire her. Even better, ask the applicant to write down five questions they want to be asked that will put them in the best light. This is straight out of Chet Holmes's book and it's something I do every time. In fact you don't even have to ask the questions, but just seeing what they wrote will be interesting and it will give you some insight.

If you do invite them in for an interview, choose a time that will work best for you, not them. How bad do they want this job, and will they show up on time for the interview? How reliable is your applicant?

I always like to have a trusted employee interview them first. To many times we tend to hire fast and fire slow, especially when we are in a small business. The fact is the slower you hire the better your candidate will be. And let's face it, your time is very valuable, so let the first interview be done by an employee, a spouse, or someone you trust. If they qualify then set up another interview for you.

THE INTERVIEW

Now we're switching gears on our new applicant a little here. If you did the phone interview right they probably think you're a jerk and may be a little intimidated. Now it's time to build rapport and see how good our applicant is at building rapport.

INTERVIEW: you will say the following:

"We hire based on personality profile. Would you agree this is important?"

"Good I'd like to ask you some personal questions."

"The best thing you can do here is be yourself, don't try and give me answers I want to hear."

"Describe your childhood growing up?"

"What shaped you as a person?"

"Did you ever aspire to be anything growing up? And how did your parents react?"

One common denominator they found when interviewing giants such as Bill Gates, Donald Trump, Richard Branson, etc. was a parent of the opposite sex who wholeheartedly supported their dreams and ambitions when they were very young.

"What are some of the biggest challenges in your life?"

"What are your area's of accomplishment?"

"What was the toughest sale you ever made?"

"Tell me about a time in your life when the odds were stacked against you but you overcame."

"Tell me 3 things you are most proud of."

"Have you ever reached a high level beyond just getting by?"

"How would your best friend describe you?"

I love this question because it helps them to say good stuff about themselves without coming across as arrogant.

"Who has the most faith in you? Why?

"What is your best memories?

"Rate yourself one-to-ten in these areas.

1. Ambition
2). Confidence
3. Ability to face rejection
4. Establishing Rapport
5. Qualifying Skills
6. Ability to Create desire in your prospects
7. Closing the Sale
8. Time Management
9. Decorating Skills
10. Strategic Thinking
11. Market Knowledge
12. Self-Improvement: Do you have any books on sale?

When they rate themselves you want someone who is a 9 or 10 in every category. That shows ego and that shows that they believe in themselves.

"Who's the best salesperson you know?"

"What makes him better than you?"

"Tell me about a disagreement you had with your last boss."

"Name two weak points of your last boss."

"Name two times a supervisor criticized you."

The 3rd and 4th questions are also favorites of mine. How did they criticize their last boss? Did they feel it was something their boss or company was doing wrong. How much do they care about the success of the company? If they have some criticisms because they believe the company could have done better that is someone you want working for you.

Now if they are truly a superstar with good rapport building skills and a healthy ego, you should be able to get them for straight commission. A great salesperson will make a lot more money on straight commission then someone who is relying on a salary.

You just finished your interview with Mary and you've decided that you like her and you want to hire her.

> You: *"Well thanks for coming in today Mary, you seem to be a wonderful person with good skills but I'm not sure if you can handle this position."*

> Mary: *"What do you mean by that?"*

> You: *"Well, remember where you said you never sold in a customer's home before? It's difficult and I'm not sure if you are cut out for this type of work."*

OK, now Mary's getting pissed and a little defensive. Strong Ego right?

> Mary: *"I can handle home sales, in fact I could probably out sell you!"*

> You: *"The problem is this Mary, this job is straight commission. You won't make any money unless you can sell and I'm afraid you might get out there and not be able to close. No offense but I don't think you are cut out for this."*

You really got under Mary's skin with this one. She has a strong ego and damn it she's going to prove you wrong!

> Mary: *"I can do it. I don't care if it's straight commission,*

give me the job and I'll prove you wrong."

You: *"All right, I tell you what, why don't you come in next Monday and let's give it a shot."*

There. You just hired Mary for straight commission.

Hiring new people is difficult no matter which system you are using. Finding and hiring straight commission people is really difficult but it can be done.

Another way I've hired people in the past is by giving them a two-month draw against their commissions. When I do this I lay down clear and specific expectations.

In order to earn your draw you must:

1. Attend regular meetings.
2. Get ongoing product training.
3). Join 2 networking groups.
4. Hand out door hangers.
5. Work every other Saturday in the showroom.
6. Go on at least 20 in-home estimates per month.

By the time the two months are up I should be able to make enough money to cover their draw, or I will have enough information to let them go. If you can't close sales up to industry standards, then you're in the wrong field.

HOW DO YOU KEEP AND MAINTAIN GOOD EMPLOYEES?

Another question could be, *"How do you make employees great and keep them?"*

Someone asked me the other day, "Do you think if we paid Susie more money we would get more out of her?"

Answer: NO!

Money is not as big of a motivator as people think it is. The people who do a good job either inheritably have a great work ethic, or they have employers who lay down specific expectations and design systems to make a company operate better.

We have two major gas stations in Phoenix, AZ. One is Circle K. They've been in this market as long as I can remember. Maybe since oil was invented? The other company is QT – Quick Trip. They are the new kids on the block and they're crushing all other gas stations, including Circle K.

When you go into QT the people behind the counter always great you, shouting out a "HELLO!" At first it was a bit annoying, but after a while if you went in and no one greeted you it made you wonder, *"Hey where's my Hello?"* The stores are always clean, the staff is friendly, and the experience is much better than Circle K.

My question to you is this: *Does QT hire better employees than Circle K?* Most people believe they do, but that's not true. QT does a much better job training their employees. Employees are like monkeys – which may offend some of you but it's the truth. You have to train your monkey to act human. You have to train them how to answer the phone, greet a customer, ask that customer for information, sell, dress, and behave.

The reason most business owners fail is because they don't take the time or make the effort to train their monkeys. You must train people if you expect them to succeed. You need to set up a system to train your employees so they understand the culture, the goals, the mission statement, how you expect them to treat customers, and they need to know that you care very much about your business.

If you train your employees with a lot of heart, excitement, and enthusiasm they will catch the bug and they will be excited to be a part of something great.

The next thing your employees need is *crystal clear expectations.* You need to tell them what you expect them to do and what you want them to accomplish. You need to give them goals and make sure they are setting goals for themselves. You want them to be excited about creating, working towards, and accomplishing their goals.

Now just because you lay down proper expectations and you set systems in place both verbally and on paper doesn't mean you shouldn't reinforce that. I've always been amazed how I could have a conversation with a 47 year old employee and it sounds similar to the conversation I had with my 12 year old son. You have to tell your employees what you expect of them more than once. Yes I know they are adults, but that's the way it is. If you understand that you can avoid being frustrated. A big key to your happiness is knowing what to expect and don't get frustrated when you have to repeat yourself.

———— EXERCISE ————

Take a second now and write down what you expect of your employees. If they are doing their jobs to the best of their ability, what would that look like?

_____

_____

_____

_____

_____

_____

_____

_____

_____

_____

_____

Here's where the rubber meets the road. You need to have the courage to fire a bad employee. For some people they just can't handle the thought of firing someone. This is where you need to show true leadership. This is where you need to prove that you respect yourself and you respect your efforts. This is where you show the character and pride in the business you are running. This is where you say, *"Dammit I'm working my butt off 12 hours a day six days a week and I'll be damned if I will let someone ruin what I'm building!"*

You are just working too hard and you are taking to many risks to hang on to a bad employee.

If you have kids you know what it's like to threaten your kid with a punishment of spanking or grounding and you don't follow thru with that threat. After a few times your kids understand that you're really not going to punish them and they won't behave after a threat. Your employees will behave the same. If you lay down proper expectations, such as showing up on time, or staying on their cell phone during office hours, or changing their attitude, and they still show up 15 minutes late to work, or is still texting during the time they should be calling customers, or their attitude is still lousy and it's affecting the way others behave, *then you have to FIRE that person.*

You were fair, you told them what the problem was and how to correct it. You gave your employee a fair chance at success and that's all you are obligated to do.

Have you ever watched one of those restaurant shows where they chew out the employees and even fire one? Did you notice how everyone falls in line so they don't lose their job? Not only that, they actually like their job more and take pride in taking better care of their customers.

Now, if you do fire someone it's important to be clear as to why, and if you can give them advice on how they can perform better at their next job then you should help them. I also think you should allow him the opportunity to say whatever they want without you defending yourself. Let them get anything off their chest to walk away with a clear conscience. It's a healthy exercise for both of you.

What's worse than firing a bad employee? *EXTINCTION!*

This is something I read in the book called *Magic Kingdom* by Tom Connellan. He writes, the worst thing you can do to an employee is give them no feedback. I worked for a guy that was like that once. It was a van conversion shop and I did upholstery. The owner paid us well but never spoke to us. He wouldn't tell us we were doing a good job or thank us for meeting a deadline. He also wouldn't yell at us for screwing up or working to slow.

If you don't give your employees any feedback they are left to their own imagination. Believe me they won't be feeling the love either. They're going to be wondering all the time if you are pissed off and if you're going to fire them. That attitude is going to affect their performance and, quite possibly, they may quit and go to work for someone who pays them less, but appreciates them more.

CHAPTER

6

GET THE MOST OUT OF YOUR EMPLOYEES AND YOURSELF

Weekly Meetings

DO NOT DISMISS THIS CHAPTER!

EVEN IF You are a one- or two-person operation.

A weekly meeting gives you and your team an opportunity to really work on the growth and success of your business. This is when you will cover many general business topics.

1. Discuss systems for selling. *How can you and your team improve?*

2. Tell your salespeople which ads are running and which promotions you are running. A lot of employers don't do this and it's very frustrating for the sales team.

3. Have your team set their goals during the meeting and track their progress.

4. Give special recognition to someone doing well. Encourage someone who needs it. Don't beret anyone in front of the team. Now's not the time for that.

5. Discuss how employees can improve the way they're answering the phones or greeting customers as they walk in the door.

6. Discuss the current problems going on. During the week I like to handle the problem but bring it up during the meeting so we can discuss a system for handling problems.

7. Go over one of your products each month. Constant education helps everyone's performance, from the person answering the phone to the salespeople, and even the owner. Stay on one product for a whole month so your team knows that product better than any of your competition.

RULES FOR YOUR MEETINGS

1) Make sure your meetings don't turn into a bitch session. Make sure you stay in control of your meetings and keep them moving. Don't let people whine and complain. I've always told my employees I'm really not interested in hearing about problems unless they've thought of a solution. Engage your employees to come up with ideas, get them involved.

2) Be prepared for your meeting. It's best to plan an agenda but I've always kept a basic plan in case I didn't have time to plan. There is always four or five topics that I will discuss with my team. That's my little fail-safe in case I don't plan.

3) Make sure your meetings are at least once a week. Many people feel that two times a month is enough or that even once a month is enough. Have you ever been involved in a networking group? The ones that meet every week get much better results than the ones who meet one or twotimes a month. It's like working out. If you exercise three or four times a week you will get much better results than if you were to exercise once a week.

4) Choose a day and time and make it mandatory. It's like

any other appointment for your employees. If you have a Tuesday meeting at 8 a.m., make it mandatory for everyone to show up on time. Tell them to put it in their appointment books and don't change it for any reason. They should tell their customers they have an appointment at that time and they can contact them right after.

5) If you have multiple departments, you should have a meeting for each department. For instance I know a gentleman who owns a security screen company. He has a weekly meeting for his sales people, but he never has meetings for the men out back making the screen doors. Now, maybe they only need a 15-minute meeting, but a quick meeting to set goals, talk about quality control issues, talk about productivity, and give special recognition to someone is very valuable to the success of that business.

6) If you are only a one-man show I would suggest you get an accountability partner. Find someone you can meet with once a week for coffee or a hamburger at lunch. Discuss what is going on in your business and ways that you can improve it. Set goals and go over your progress each week.

MEASURING YOUR PROGRESS IS ONE OF THE MOST IMPORTANT THINGS YOU CAN DO.

There are a lot of one or two man operations out there so I don't want to gloss over that. The problem you have as a one person operation is that you aren't accountable to anyone except yourself. Sure you need to take care of your family and that may seem like enough motivation, but it's much easier to get something done if your boss is expecting it. Your accountability partner should expect you to hold true to your goals, and you should provide that for him/her as well.

Recently I was working with a client who said, *"Our business is not going so well right now. We've lost our motivation. I can't get the team back on track."* This is a three-man operation, so not a big company right? I asked him if he had a weekly meeting. He said, *"We used to and things were great. We got a lot done and everyone was energized and motivated, but one person had a vacation and the other one didn't want to meet without the whole team so we just stopped having weekly meetings."* I didn't have to suggest to him to get back to the weekly meetings, he heard himself and created a goal to get back to it.

Without that dedicated time to focus on improving your business you will be left constantly reacting to situations rather than controlling the outcomes.

——— EXERCISE ———

Right now! Set aside 90 minutes per week that you will dedicate to the growth of your company.

Which day will you choose? _____

What time will you choose? _____

Now I want you to choose three to five subjects that you will cover during every meeting such as:

- Reviewing current sales and specials
- Going over your products *(Choose a single product until your team gets it down.)*
- Discussing sales goals and progress
- Discussing problems and situations that came up during the week
- Recognizing a great performance

List your 3 to 5 subjects here:

1. _____

2. _____

3. _____

4. _____

5. _____

Just because you go over policies and procedures with your team, it doesn't mean you're done. Yes, I know they're adults but less face it, they have a better chance of remembering the names of the *American Idol* contestants than information you cover in the meetings. You need to go over the same subjects several times in order for people to get it, so don't be afraid to repeat some subjects in your meetings.

A Word Of Caution!

You *will* miss a meeting or two. You *will* stop having them at some point for one reason or another. That's OK, it happens. Once you realize that is happening, you need to get back to it. Get back to the meetings that did work in the past and get everyone back on board.

Overall you will see a great improvement in your entire team; better communication, a better understanding of each other, and a better desire to be a part of a growing company. Your employees will be engaged and excited to be a part of your success story, rather than just someone who has a job and can't wait for the weekends.

—— WHAT I'VE LEARNED ——

PUT IT
ALL TOGETHER

The Right Attitude

I've considered whether or not this chapter should be first or last. My concern is that it may be too nuanced and "fu-fu" for people who are anxious to grow and improve their business.

Your attitude MEANS EVERYTHING when you are trying to succeed or simply enjoy life and be happy. How can you have a good attitude? *No, really.* How the hell are you supposed to be happy during times of stress, trial, and tribulation?

- Overdue bills

- Can't pay suppliers on time!

- Can't figure out your marketing plan or sales plan

- Employees are a pain in the ass!

- Maybe your marriage has been rough

- Your kids teacher just sent a note home, and it didn't say how great Johnny was behaving in school.

- Did you hear about the accident on the news today where kids died?

- Man I'm sick and tired of this traffic!

How am I going to make enough money to pay my bills, save for the future, pay my employees, and live a happy successful life?

With all of these outside forces and influences on your brain, how are you supposed to be a happy productive person? On top of all that you just aren't that lucky, are you? I mean you're no Bill Gates, or Donald Trump. They've got it easy. They're so rich and successful; and it was easy for them.

In fact now would be a good time to write down all the reasons that you are having trouble succeeding in your business and your life. Get them all down on paper and let's deal with the problems. Stop right now and do this exercise.

———— EXERCISE ————

Write down all your problems below:

_____

_____

_____

_____

_____

_____

_____

_____

_____

_____

_____

_____

_____

_____

I hope it felt good to get it all out. You acknowledged the reasons you feel you struggle and you put it down on paper.

NOW STOP WITH ALL THE EXECUSES!

Every time you make an excuse you are giving up control over your life. If you blame the economy then you trap yourself into economic conditions. If you blame the President, then you are giving him, (maybe her by the time you read this) control over your life. If you blame your family, then you're making yourself a slave who is not in control of your own destiny. Why would you ever allow yourself to be a prisoner in your own life?

Don't ever give anyone, especially yourself, any more reasons why you can't accomplish your goals and your dreams. Never EVER say, *"I can't."* You need to say, *"How can I?"*

The faster you realize that you have to depend on yourself first, the quicker you can accept responsibility for your own situation, and the faster you'll be able to take positive action. The next time you are in front of a mirror I want you to look hard at yourself. The person staring back at you is the one you can count on the most. There is no white knight coming to save you. You can get help from others, but unless you are willing to fight to help yourself, unless you are determined to succeed, unless you are willing to dream big and have big desires, no one will be able to help you.

Accepting full responsibility for your life and your attitude is the first step in changing your situation. I read an interesting story in Darren Hardy's book, *The Compound Effect.* The question he possess is how responsible are you for your marriage? Is it 50 percent, 51 percent, 75 percent? No, the real answer is 100 percent. You are 100 percent responsible and that's with 0 percent expectation of getting anything in return. That's a hard one to grasp, isn't it? But think about it, if you take 100 percent responsibility for your marriage without having any expectations in return, how do you believe your spouse will respond?

Darren Hardy goes on to explain how he took this advice to heart and every day for a year he would write down something special his wife did that made him smile. He wrote it down in a journal and on Thanksgiving day, he gave it to her. It was the best gift she ever received. She was so grateful that she, too, made greater efforts to become a better wife. The other thing that happened is that Darren's attitude about his wife began to change. His love for her grew greater every day. He started to appreciate her more by taking 100 percent responsibility.

You have to take 100 percent responsibility in every relationship and every situation in order to control your life and your happiness. Sometimes the choice you make is to not have a relationship with people who bring you down. You can only control YOU, so if someone around you is bringing you down then you may have to stop seeing him or her.

CONTROL YOUR ENVIRONMENT

I had an employee working for me who would always seem to get into trouble. He even had a roommate who committed suicide. It wasn't his fault but he always had chaos in his life. In fact I nick-named him "Captain Chaos." I even told him this when I wanted to give him a second chance. I liked the guy but his attitude and lifestyle were destructive and I was working my but off trying to run a successful business. I ended up firing him because I wasn't going to allow his attraction for chaos to come into my business or my environment.

I'm sure this isn't the only book you've read on business and personal growth and success. Wouldn't it be better to surround yourself with those who are reading the same books, attending Master Mind groups, and making the effort to live better lives? I enjoy going to the bar with friends or a baseball game, but if someone is going to complain about their work, their marriage, their car, and life in general, then that person is sucking positive energy out of my life and, I'm sorry but, I'm not interested.

It's okay to complain about a situation going on in your life, but if you aren't trying to overcome the problem and come up with a solution, then you'll end up being the type of person no one wants to hang out with, and you will attract more problems and more complainers.

FAMILY OPPORTUNITIES

Now it's really tough when the complainers are in your family. If your parents are complaining all the time, obviously you aren't just going to cut Mom out of your life, but you may end up seeing her less. If it's your brother or sister who is whining all the time, it makes it tougher but you will have to try and control your environment. What about your kids?

Here's where the real opportunity lies. If your kids are still young you will find it easier to help give them a positive happy attitude. When you read books about success it changes the way you raise your children. Now, my kids still whine and complain once in awhile like most children, but my wife and I are always working to change how they think about things and we don't put up with the whining. Not because it's annoying, because we want them to grow up with the habit of trying to live a happy life.

THE 30-DAY DIET

One of the things you can do to have the greatest impact on your attitude is to go on a 30-Day Diet. My diets are awesome because you can still eat anything you want. I want you to go on a "News Diet." In fact I want you to go on a "TV Diet." If you really want to turn your life around quickly, then this shouldn't be too hard. You absolutely should cut out the news for one month and replace it with positive tapes by Tony Robbins,

Chet Holmes, Dan Kennedy, *Success Magazine,* Joe Polish, or anything you can get your hands on. You don't have to buy these CDs new, you can get them cheap on Amazon or Craig's List, or borrow them from a friend.

The news does not serve you well. Learning about a mother who drowned her kids or the latest car accident does not benefit you in any way. The latest political scandal is interesting, but it's also frustrating and will provide you no benefit in serving your customer.

TV shows also have an enormous influence on our mental health. I remember when I went thru my divorce I started watching *Friends* and *Seinfield* a lot. My attitude started becoming that sex was a casual thing people did and it was no big deal. Now I enjoyed both shows and they were very funny, but they did influence the way I thought about society? The shows you are watching now will influence the way you think.

Can you commit to the 30-day diet?

Circle one: Yes   or   Yes

I _____ promise to cut out the news and all shows and movies that may have a negative influence on my attitude.

Start date: _____/_____/_____

HEALTH

How you feel will have a big influence over your attitude and your energy. I'm not big on health issues so I'm not going to pretend to know a lot about how you should take care of yourself. But I do know that being overweight does influence how you feel and work and getting in shape will have a positive influence on the way you think and feel.

I personally believe that the best way to live a long and happy life is to control the amount of stress you have in your life. Dennis Prager does a daytime radio talk show, and every year he does one show where he talks to people who are very old to find out how they've lived so long. Most of them haven't taken good care of themselves. Some still smoke and some still drink. The biggest reason they give for living so long is that they are happy, stress-free people. They love life and they enjoy living it.

Everyone has their own formula for living a healthy life so you need to find out what works for you. My own personal opinion is, stay away from health magazines. According to those magazines, Diet Coke will kill you, as will milk, cookies, crackers, walking, running too fast, breathing our air, drinking the water, etc., etc. They talk about all the things that are bad for you and if you were to cut them out you would live forever. I believe all they do is add stress and worry to your life, and in the end, they don't improve the quality of your life. *(But that's just this author's personal opinion.)*

DON'T BEAT YOURSELF UP!

I just love raising my kids. I'm like everyone else who wants to do a better job than their parents. That's very difficult in my case since my parents gave me an outstanding childhood, but still, you don't want to end up sounding like them. One thing I hated more than anything else as a kid was when someone said, *"You don't listen."* Just because I didn't do what you advised me to do doesn't mean I didn't listen; it just means I made a different choice.

I never tell my kids, "You don't listen", because I know it's easy to tell someone what to do but it's not always easy to take advice. Everyone has to make decisions for themselves, especially if they are to remain in control of their lives. I give my son advice all the time and it's up to him to decide what he should do.

Making mistakes is a big part of life. I expect my kids to make a lot of mistakes and do a lot of stupid things. You will learn a whole lot more from your own mistakes then you will from others'. The important thing to remember is to learn from your mistakes and **Don't Beat Yourself Up!**

Everyone does stupid stuff, whether it's making a bad decision to buy a car, getting into debt, going thru a bad marriage or divorce; maybe you even committed a crime, or went to jail, God forbid! The point is we all do things we regret and we all do things we shouldn't have. So, how do you plan to live the rest of your life?

This book was written to help business people succeed and, even in business, we do things we wished we hadn't. And everyone who owns a business has a personal life to deal with. You can be successful in your business and fail in your marriage but the goal in life should be to be a happy person.

Every week Dennis Prager does *The Happiness Hour* on Friday afternoons. He says you have a responsibility to act happy. It's very interesting isn't it? He doesn't say you have a responsibility to *be* happy but he feels you must *act* happy. You owe it to yourself, and the people around you.

My main goal in life is to be happy. One thing that bothers me more than anything else is when I allow a person or situation to affect the way I feel. I hate to give up control to someone else.

All your goals can be achieved without happiness, but they are a lot more difficult to accomplish. Furthermore, what would be the point of reaching your goals if you weren't happy?

———— WHAT I'VE LEARNED ————

JERRY LEVINSON

I was born and raised in Phoenix, AZ. When I was a kid, I stepped on the lawn of a witch in our neighborhood and she put a curse on me. She said I would always live in Arizona, and I could only move in August. (*That's a little secret I kept from my wife until she married me.*)

I'm one of six boys in our family. My older brothers and younger brothers are twins and not anything alike in looks or personalities. My childhood was excellent and my goal in life is to give my kids the kind of childhood that my parents gave us.

I love life, I love business, and I'm fortunate to have achieved my goals of creating a well-run, profitable business, Blind Devotion, and sell it. My bigger goal was to provide consulting, which I am now doing full time and loving it.

This is supposed to be about the author and not a solicitation but the truth is I do love working with people to help them get the most out of their marketing, employees, sales process, and business as a whole. I am doing what I love so it's hard to call it work.

Life is full of fantastic opportunities. I hope you are working towards the goals that make you feel great to wake up every day, and even better when you are working until 1 a.m.

www.ingramcontent.com/pod-product-compliance
Lightning Source LLC
Chambersburg PA
CBHW050513210326
41521CB00011B/2434